The Whole Armor of God

C. David Belt

With a foreword by
Eric D. Huntsman, PhD.

Photography:
Olya Polazhynets Goodrick

Legionnaire:
Jacob M. Belt

Copyright 2018 C. David Belt

ISBN (paperback): 978-1-5136-4357-1

ISBN (ebook): 978-0-4635-8888-8

PARABLES

Walkersville, MD

http://www.parablespub.com

parables@parablespub.com

Table of Contents

Foreword: Onward, Christian Soldiers!	9
Introduction: The Whole Armour of God	11
Chapter I: Cingulum Militare	16
Chapter II: Lorica Segmentata	22
Chapter III: Caligae	28
Chapter IV: Scutum	34
Chapter V: Galea	40
Chapter VI: Gladius	45
Conclusion: Stand!	51
Acknowledgments	55

Foreword: Onward Christian Soldiers

As a lover of history and an expert on ancient weaponry, David Belt is certainly qualified to explicate for us Paul's well-known injunction that we "put on the whole armour of God" (*King James Bible*, Ephesians 6:11-17). In this interesting and vividly illustrated volume, he ably describes for us what the various implements that Paul mentions—such as the breastplate, shield, and helmet—would have looked like and how they would have functioned in Paul's time. But more importantly, he explains the spiritual significance of Paul's imagery, drawing widely upon the scriptures and some of his own experiences to help us better understand how we can spiritually fortify ourselves to fight the most important battles in our own lives.

As David Belt so carefully demonstrates, the detailed description of each item in the panoply, or full suit of armor, comes from the standard issue worn by Roman legionaries, the most effective and feared soldiers of the time. At first Paul's appropriation of Roman armor seems unexpected: were not the Romans the enemies of the Christians? Actually, no. While local opposition, first from some Jewish elements in the cities where Paul taught and then later from unbelieving Gentile neighbors, was seen from the outset, by and large the Roman government was surprisingly tolerant, and Paul, as a Roman citizen, often benefited from the protection of local Roman officials. Only with the burning of Rome in A.D. 64, a disaster that the emperor Nero chose to blame on local Christians, did periodic waves of persecution begin, including the round that seems to have claimed both Peter and Paul.

Yet even when the Roman state, as represented by its military, was ranged against individual believers or groups of Christians, for Paul the real enemy was never Rome. Rome, Babylon, and the other ancient empires before it and dictators and genocidal regimes since were, are, and always will be only the front men for the true enemy of the saints. As the hosts of Satan continued their perennial war against the faithful, the defensive armor *and* the offensive potential of the legions of Christ could best be characterized in the minds of first century Christians by the best military equipment they knew. "With the cross of Jesus, going on before,"

The Whole Armor of God

the peaceable followers of Christ were assured that they were, in fact, part of a victorious army of the righteous, and that was an image that Paul returned to in several of his letters to the early saints.

Ephesians, which has the most detailed use of this military image, is one of the later letters attributed to Paul, perhaps written between A.D. 61–63 from Rome. Armor imagery, however, was not new to the Pauline corpus, appearing in perhaps the earliest letter of Paul, which he wrote to the Thessalonians in A.D. 50 or 51. At that time Paul and many of his converts apparently expected the return of Jesus Christ to be imminent. While Paul reminded the Thessalonians that the promised day of the Lord "cometh as a thief in the night" (*King James Bible*, 1 Thessalonians 5:2), he repeatedly urged them to be ready so that they would be numbered among "the children of light" who would be on the Lord's side at his return. Although the Thessalonians were Greeks, Paul drew heavily upon the Hebrew Bible for his apocalyptic imagery, reassuring these new converts, who had been suffering so much at the hands of unbelievers, that the Lord would defend and vindicate them if only they were ready and prepared at his coming. With that in mind he enjoined, "But let us, who are of the day, be sober, putting on the breastplate of faith and love; and for an helmet, the hope of salvation" (*King James Bible*, 1 Thessalonians 5:8).

Paul's image of a breastplate and helmet may well have come from Isaiah 59:17, where the LORD, or Jehovah, is described donning "righteousness as a breastplate, and an helmet of salvation upon his head; and he put on the garments of vengeance for clothing, and was clad with zeal as a cloak." Because latter-day saints understand that this same Jehovah was the premortal Christ, the next lines in Paul's warning to the Thessalonians takes on added meaning: they should put on the breastplate of faith and love and the hope of salvation, "For God hath not appointed us to wrath, but to obtain salvation by our Lord Jesus Christ, Who died for us, that, whether we wake or sleep, we should live together with him" (*King James Bible*, 1 Thessalonians 5:9–10). While the great and terrible day of the Lord would be a terrible day of wrath for the wicked, it will be a great day of salvation for the saints who put on the same armor that Isaiah had foreseen their Savior wearing when He came to rescue them. In other words, to be saved they needed to, as we must, put on Christ, being clothed in His righteousness and receiving His salvation.

C. David Belt

In his later letter to the Corinthians, Paul again took up this image of Christ's righteousness as armor that a servant of Christ put on as protection against evil. Yet in this letter, written some six years later than 1 Thessalonians, Paul was not thinking as much about the final battle as he was the regular, daily struggles that saints face in this life. Writing of how he and other true apostles had been and would be defended by the Lord until they finished their work, he testified,

> **But in all things approving ourselves as the ministers of God, in much patience, in afflictions, in necessities, in distresses, In stripes, in imprisonments, in tumults, in labours, in watchings, in fastings; By pureness, by knowledge, by longsuffering, by kindness, by the Holy Ghost, by love unfeigned, By the word of truth, by the power of God,** *by the armour of righteousness* **on the right hand and on the left . . .** (*King James Bible*, 2 Corinthians 6:4–7, *emphasis added*)

Then again in Romans, written probably about A.D. 57 or 58 from Corinth, Paul returned to the image of armor, again in the current struggle against the world and its temptations. Rather than focusing on the final, ultimate rescue that would come at Christ's return, Paul spoke of salvation *now*, salvation that would require that we put on Christ at this moment, "knowing the time, that now it is high time to awake out of sleep: for now, is our salvation nearer than when we believed. The night is far spent, the day is at hand: let us therefore cast off the works of darkness, and let us put on the armour of light" (*King James Bible*, Romans 13:11–12).

Finally, toward the end of his ministry and not long perhaps before his own martyrdom for the truth of Christ, Paul wrote his most fulsome use of armor imagery to the Ephesians, directly targeted at defending saints from the power of the true enemy, Satan:

> **Finally, my brethren, be strong in the Lord, and in the power of his might. Put on the whole armour of God, that ye may be able to stand against the wiles of the devil. For we wrestle not against flesh and blood, but against principalities, against powers, against the rulers**

The Whole Armor of God

of the darkness of this world, against spiritual wickedness in high places. Wherefore take unto you the whole armour of God, that ye may be able to withstand in the evil day, and having done all, to stand. (*King James Bible*, Ephesians 6:10–13)

As we read the detailed description and discussion of each piece of this armor that follows in this wonderfully illustrated volume, it is good to keep in mind Paul's repeated use of such imagery in his writings. Whether it referred to our daily struggles against temptation and life's trials or points us forward to the final confrontation with Satan and his hosts, we should remember that the image of such armor began with Isaiah's description of Jehovah arming Himself to fight on behalf of His people. As we join the ranks of Christian soldiers in putting on Jesus' righteousness and fighting in His ranks, we can remember the lines of the familiar hymn:

Onward, Christian soldiers!
Marching as to war,
With the cross of Jesus
Going on before.
Christ, the royal Master,
Leads against the foe;
Forward into battle,
See his banners go!

Like a mighty army
Moves the Church of God;
Brothers, we are treading
Where the Saints have trod.
We are not divided;
All one body we:
One in hope and doctrine,
One in charity.

Onward, Christian soldiers!
Marching as to war,
With the cross of Jesus
Going on before.[1]

Eric D. Huntsman, PhD
Brigham Young University

---

1 "Onward Christian Soldiers," *Hymns* no. 246, vv. 1 and 2.

Introduction:
The Whole Armour of God

"Put on the whole armour of God, that ye may be able to stand against the wiles of the devil. For we wrestle not against flesh and blood, but against principalities, against powers, against the rulers of the darkness of this world, against spiritual wickedness in high places. Wherefore take unto you the whole armour of God, that ye may be able to withstand in the evil day, and having done all, to stand." (*King James Bible*, Ephesians 6:11–13)

I remember the night I was baptized. I was eight years old. I lived with my parents in the Philippines, and I was baptized in the base pool at Clark Air Force Base.

I remember I caught a frog that night. I found the tiny creature in the grass beside the pool. I remember that my mother forgot to bring an extra pair of underwear for me, so I had to spend the rest of the evening "going commando" (although we didn't call it that back then). After the baptism, my parents took me to see Disney's *Follow Me, Boys!* on an outdoor screen at "The Bamboo Bowl" (the base football field). I remember that it was uncomfortable sitting for hours on the bleachers, watching the movie, with nothing more than my thin pants between the rough, wooden bench and my poor, tender bottom.

The Whole Armor of God

What I don't remember is virtually anything about the baptism itself. I don't remember wearing white. I don't remember holding on to my father's forearm as he grasped my wrist gently but firmly. I don't remember my father raising his arm to the square and speaking the sacred words of the baptismal ordinance. I don't even remember being dunked in the water.

At the time, I missed all the rich symbolism in the ordinance: death and rebirth, burial and resurrection, the washing away of sins, the Atonement of Jesus Christ. I focused on the wrong things. Granted, I was *eight*, but I wish I could've remembered what was truly meaningful about that special night long ago.

I don't even remember what happened to the frog.

C. David Belt

Today, when referring to Paul's great analogy of the "whole armour of God," we tend to employ medieval European imagery. We often picture a "knight in shining armor," wearing a polished and gleaming suit of plate mail, bearing a triangular shield, and carrying a great sword or a broadsword. All that is missing is a lance decorated with a Lady's favor, a huge white horse, and a plaque reading, "Sir Lancelot."

However, this was not the imagery that Paul had in mind.

After all, Paul was a Roman.

Yes, the apostle was raised as a devout Jew and later became a Christian, but he was a *citizen* of the Roman Empire. He lived in a Roman world. Being a Roman citizen granted Paul special status, since most subjects of Rome were not *citizens*. (Paul's Roman citizenship, for example, allowed

The Whole Armor of God

him to appeal to Caesar to avoid being handed over to the Jews for a mock trial and certain execution by stoning.)

In his Epistle to the Ephesians, Paul wrote to an audience of Christians living in a Roman world. There is some debate as to whether Ephesians was written specifically to the saints at Ephesus (the words "in Ephesus" are not present in the first verse of the earliest manuscripts) or to the early Church as a whole. But whoever they were, Paul's audience lived under Roman rule. They had all seen Roman legionnaires and were familiar with the armor and weapons (hopefully, from a safe distance) carried by a typical Roman soldier.

I emphasize this point, because, when it comes to the "whole armour of God," I think that, as contemporary Christians, Latter-day Saint or otherwise, we are using the wrong imagery. We miss the powerful symbolism of Paul's analogy. There is deep meaning in each of the symbols that Paul uses—symbols that we gloss over or fail entirely to understand.

When the Lord repeats Himself, it behooves us to take special notice. The analogy and imagery of the "whole armour of God" is important enough that the Lord reiterated it in D&C Section 27.

I think back to when I was baptized by one bearing the holy priesthood: I wore white, was immersed under the water, had my sins washed clean, and was born again. And after that great and life-altering experience of eternal consequence, my most vivid memory of that sacred ordinance concerned a frog.

So, rather than picturing a Lancelot or a Percival, let us visualize instead a Roman legionnaire, just as Paul did.

In the following chapters, we will discuss the various parts of the "armour of God" and the rich symbolism they are meant to convey. Please understand that I am **not** glorifying Rome or the Roman army. I am merely employing the same inspired imagery that Paul used. Unlike the Roman army, we are not trying to conquer or enslave or subdue; we

The Whole Armor of God

are striving to stand strong in the gospel of Jesus Christ and to be instruments in bringing souls to Him. We fight, not to control men, but to free them. And, perhaps more importantly, we fight to remain true to our Savior.

Before we examine the items in the whole armor of God which help us to "withstand in the evil day," please allow me to point out one item that the Roman soldier wore which Paul does **not** mention but is implicit: the tunic. There is symbolism there as well.

The *tunica* (tunic) of the Roman soldier was dyed crimson. This custom of dying the *tunica* red was borrowed from the Spartans, a famous martial race of ancient Greece. The *tunica* was red so that the enemy would not see a Roman bleed. Blood and sweat look virtually the same on the *tunica*: a dark, wet patch of red. This was calculated to hide weakness and promote courage among the Roman ranks. The time to worry about wounds was *after* the battle was won, not while a soldier was busy fighting it.

Until victory was achieved, a soldier was expected to stand his ground and fight on.

The red of the *tunica* might also represent the blood of the Savior. In ancient times, a legionnaire ritually showered in the blood of a sacrificial bull before going into combat. This was meant to give him courage and protection in battle and to cleanse him of sin, so that, if he fell in combat, he would die sinless. Likewise, the atoning blood of Jesus Christ washes us clean and protects us from spiritual death when we venture into spiritual combat.

Chapter I: Cingulum Militare

"Stand therefore, having your loins girt about with truth" (*King James Bible*, Ephesians 6:14)

Within a Roman military unit, all soldiers wore the same armor. Once an armored legionnaire put on the *galea* (helmet) and tied its cheek guards under his chin, his hair was covered, and his face was cast in shadow. He was virtually indistinguishable from the other soldiers in his unit. (Officers were distinguished by a horsehair crest or sometimes by a wolf, bear, or lion pelt worn on the top of the helmet.) The only part of the uniform that could be personalized was the *cingulum militare* (military belt). This item was a simple leather belt worn about the waist of the tunic. A variable number of leather strips (usually five) hung from the belt in front of the groin area. The *cingulum militare* was often the only means of distinguishing one fully armored soldier from another. Even when the legionnaire was not in armor, he usually wore his *cingulum militare*.

The *cingulum militare* provided no physical protection for the wearer; it was purely ornamental. (A *pugio* — a Roman dagger — could be attached to the belt, but the belt itself did not protect the soldier in any physical sense.) However, in his analogy of the armor or God, Paul mentions this item first and foremost. I believe this is significant and indicates the importance of the belt with its ornamental strips of leather. Paul uses the *cingulum militare* to represent truth.

How, then, does the *cingulum militare* represent truth? And what specific truth does it signify?

Each soldier was allowed to decorate the hanging leather strips as he chose. He might attach images of his gods or his loved ones. He might have his name written on one of the strips or the name of his father or his mother or perhaps a family motto. He might decorate the strips with war trophies or other trinkets of personal significance. In short, the *cingulum militare* was analogous to a modern-day nametag and the rows of service ribbons worn on some modern military uniforms. It was a declaration of

The Whole Armor of God

who the wearer was, what he had accomplished, what he believed, and what he held most dear.

The *cingulum militare* represented a declaration of testimony, identity, integrity, and honor. It was a proclamation of what the wearer was fighting for.

If a Roman soldier committed an act that brought disgrace upon his military unit, his *optio* (officer) took a *pugio* and sliced off the *cingulum militare* of the offending soldier. This punishment had two effects:

- It instantly transformed the soldier's masculine tunic into a woman's dress (albeit a short one), symbolically unmanning him.

- It stripped the soldier of his name and honor.

Latter-day Saint missionaries wear a nametag declaring the title and last name of the missionary and the name of the Church. The name of the Savior is shown in large, bold letters. In this way, the missionary declares that he or she is representing the Church, the Savior, and the good name of the missionary's family. Sister missionaries serving on Temple Square in Salt Lake City, Utah, also have a flag representing their native country (and thus indicating the language they speak).

C. David Belt

As members of the Tabernacle Choir at Temple Square, when we are on Temple Square or touring with the Choir and *not* wearing the Choir wardrobe, we are required to wear a nametag any time we were outside our hotel rooms. This nametag displays the pipes of the Tabernacle organ (a very recognizable symbol), the Choir member's name, and the words, "TABERNACLE CHOIR." This is a constant reminder of who we are and who we represent. I, for one, would never want to do anything that might bring dishonor on the Church or the Choir while wearing that nametag.

In the Old Testament, when David was sent to bring supplies to his older brothers who were serving in the army, he observed the Philistine giant, Goliath of Gath, challenging the military forces of Israel and mocking the Lord. When no other man dared to face Goliath in single combat, David volunteered to champion the cause of Israel and Israel's God.

Typically, when this story is retold, David is depicted as a beardless youth, unaccustomed to war. However, a more careful reading of the preceding chapters of 1st Samuel shows that David was experienced in war and knew how to handle a sword, shield, and spear. However, when King Saul offered to allow David the use of Saul's own personal armor and weapons, David demurred, saying that he had not "proven" that specific set of armor. In other words, David had never wielded that particular sword and shield, nor worn that helmet and breastplate, etc. He hadn't trained or practiced with them. In short, they were not his, and he didn't trust them. Instead, he chose to face the giant armed only with stones and a sling, weapons he used every day (*King James Bible*, 1 Samuel 17).

The Whole Armor of God

As David approached Goliath, he declared who he was and what he believed: "Then said David to the Philistine, Thou comest to me with a

sword, and with a spear, and with a shield: but I come to thee in the name of the LORD of hosts, the God of the armies of Israel, whom thou hast defied" (*King James Bible*, 1 Samuel 17:45).

So why do we need our loins girt about with truth? Regardless of whatever other armor we may bear or whatever weapons we may wield, without a firm knowledge of who we are and who we represent, we cannot possibly face our Goliaths. With that firm testimony, an unshakable sense of identity, and sure knowledge of divine potential and mission, we can go forward in courage, and none can stand against us.

Testimony is the very foundation of the whole armor of God.

Chapter II: Lorica Segmentata

"And having on the breastplate of righteousness." (*King James Bible*, Ephesians 6:14)

In ancient times, the heart was considered the seat of wisdom, understanding, and courage. (Compassion and love were thought to reside in the bowels.) The breastplate or cuirass protected the vital organs.

In Paul's day, the Roman army used three types of armor to protect the torso: the *lorica musculata*, the *lorica hamata*, and the *lorica segmentata*. These are modern terms. (None of these names were used in ancient times, and the original names are lost to history.)

The *lorica musculata* was a breastplate and backplate joined by hinges or leather straps. The *lorica musculata* was sculpted to look like an idealized male torso, complete with muscles, nipples, and a navel. It was worn by generals, imperial officers, governors, and emperors. (Gods were also frequently depicted as wearing the *lorica musculata*.) This ornate breastplate was often adorned with depictions of characters and scenes from mythology. (In the example shown here, the breastplate displays the head of the gorgon Medusa.) In many cases, the *lorica musculata* was cast in bronze or plated with gold. It was rigid and did not allow freedom of movement and was therefore impractical for use in actual combat. It made the wearer appear to be heroic and physically fit, even if the physique inside did not match. In other words, it was **deceptive**, projecting a false impression of masculine perfection.

The *lorica hamata* was a simple hauberk (metal shirt) composed of interlocking mail rings. It was worn by soldiers in Roman auxiliary units (i.e., conscripts: non-Romans drafted into military service). It was not worn by legionnaires (who were Roman citizens). It was quite flexible, but very heavy (often in excess of 50 lbs.). It provided little protection from arrows, darts, or spears. A *lorica hamata* could not be considered a "breastplate" in any sense of the word.

Neither the falsely heroic *lorica musculata* nor the *lorica hamata* are good contenders for the "breastplate of righteousness." The most likely candidate for Paul's "breastplate" is the *lorica segmentata*. The *lorica segmentata* (segmented plates) was the breastplate of the Roman legionnaire during Paul's day.

The Whole Armor of God

The *lorica segmentata* was a type of laminated or laminar armor composed of curved metal plates fashioned into overlapping bands. The metallic plates were connected by internal leather straps. The plates were black laminated soft iron on the inside and mild steel on the outside. This type of construction hardened the plates against damage without making them brittle. The girth strips were arranged around the body, overlapping downward. They surrounded the body in two halves, laced together in the front and in the back. The upper body and shoulders were protected by segmented plates that went over the shoulders. The *lorica segmentata* was very flexible and allowed the legionnaire great freedom of movement, while providing substantial protection. The armor could be separated into four collapsible parts for compact storage. Weighing in at under 20 lbs., the *lorica segmentata* was much lighter than the *lorica hamata* and the bronze or gold-plated *lorica musculata*.

C. David Belt

Though a highly effective piece of armor, the *lorica segmentata* required constant maintenance to ensure the best protection. After each march, drill, or battle, hinges needed to be tightened, straps needed to be replaced, plates needed to be cleaned and oiled. Without such repairs and attention, the armor deteriorated and fell apart.

As a youth growing up in what we used to call "the mission field" (an area with very few members of the Church), I was often mocked by my peers for my Latter-day Saint standards. Many of my peers were church-going Christians, carrying their Bibles at school, sporting conspicuous crucifixes, and driving cars with bumper stickers that read, "I'm saved. R U?" and "Warning: In case of the Rapture, this car will suddenly be unoccupied!" I was mocked for striving to keep the commandments of God, such as the Word of Wisdom and the Law of Chastity. My peers saw the prohibition against drinking, smoking, drugs, and

The Whole Armor of God

premarital sex as being restrictive and limiting. They said that I wasn't free to "have a good time." In their churches, they were taught chastity and abstinence from liquor and drugs, but they regarded these teachings as guidelines rather than commandments.

Many of my peers indulged, and they reaped the fruits of their indulgence. One of my friends was a part-time youth pastor in his church. He wanted to attend a divinity college and pursue a career as a pastor. He told me that he loved nothing more than preaching and singing in his church. His pastor endorsed his application for a prestigious divinity school, and he received a scholarship from that school. He was on his way to realizing his dream. However, when his girlfriend became pregnant, his admission to divinity school was rescinded. He lost his scholarship and the **option** to pursue his dream. At eighteen years of age, he was forced to abandon his dream and take a minimum-wage job, so he could support his child.

For my part, I wrapped the commandments around myself like armor. I knew what the standard was. I knew, "This is the line that I shall not cross." The commandments and my obedience to them protected me. I was still free to drink and smoke, try marijuana, or indulge in sexual immorality—I still had the **choice** to partake—but by abstaining from those vices, I was able to avoid the consequences of such actions. I was *free* from addiction, from trouble with the law, from unwed parenthood. When I graduated from high school, I was free to serve a mission, marry in the temple, and pursue an Air Force career that required a top-secret security clearance. By choosing to obey the commandments, I had more options, more choices. I was also very aware that I had to be ever vigilant—constantly repenting, striving to improve, never becoming complacent. In other words, like the *lorica segmentata*, the breastplate of righteousness protects and enables flexibility. It is not a flashy or a vain declaration of pretended valor and piety (like the *lorica musculata*). Unlike

the *lorica hamata*, it is not a burden, weighing us down while providing little protection from the pointed threats of the enemy. And like the *lorica segmentata*, the breastplate of righteousness requires constant maintenance and repair.

In the end, however, our own personal righteousness cannot protect us without the Atonement of Jesus Christ. Our Savior lived a sinless life in mortality. His righteousness allowed Him to perform that perfect atonement for our sins. Therefore, it is only through His righteousness that we are enabled to repent and become perfected in Him.

Chapter III: Caligae

"And your feet shod with the preparation of the gospel of peace." (*King James Bible*, Ephesians 6:15)

The *caligae* were the military footwear worn by both the Roman legionnaire and the Roman auxiliary soldier. While the *caligae* resemble modern sandals, they were actually marching boots. (In ancient Rome, sandals were considered indoor footwear and were never worn outside.) A *caliga* had a hard-leather sole, studded with iron hobnails. The nails provided reinforcement for the sole and traction while marching. The top of the boot was open to allow the free passage of air. This open design helped to prevent disabling foot conditions such as blisters, tinea (a.k.a. ringworm), and trench foot. The *caligae* were worn without socks unless the army was operating in a colder climate (such as in Britain). The Roman infantry was the most mobile force of foot soldiers in the ancient world, due in large part to the *caligae*.

The prophet Isaiah said, "How beautiful upon the mountains are the *feet* of him that bringeth good tidings, that publisheth peace; that bringeth good tidings of good, that publisheth salvation; that sayeth unto Zion, Thy God reigneth" (*King James Bible*, Isaiah 52:7, *emphasis added*)! Why "the feet?" What do the feet have to do with publishing peace, bringing good tidings of good (i.e., the gospel), publishing salvation, and declaring unto Zion that God reigns? The feet themselves do not carry the good news of the gospel, but they do carry the messenger. The feet represent the ability to

The Whole Armor of God

travel so that we can declare peace, repentance, and redemption. The shoes protect the feet of the spiritual warrior.

If the shoes protect the feet and enable the Christian soldier to move quickly and safely, why does Paul mention "the *preparation* of the gospel of peace?"

Battles are only *partially* won on the battlefield itself. Most of the time, battles are won largely *before* the fighting begins. Most of an army's working time is spent in marching and maneuvering, i.e., in getting from place to place. Soldiers spend long hours in drilling and marching, because it is essential that the army be where it needs to be, when it needs to be there. And once the army gets where it needs to be, it is vital that it be healthy and be able to stand its ground.

In A.D. 60 or 61 (the exact date is not certain), a Celtic queen named Boudicca led her tribe, the Iceni, and other Celtic tribes in a rebellion to throw off the oppressive yoke of Roman rule in Britannia. Boudicca led an army of 230,000 Celts and destroyed Camulodunum (modern-day Colchester). She then marched on Londinium (modern-day London). The Roman governor Gaius Suetonius Paulinus was leading a military campaign in Cambria (Wales) when he learned of the uprising. He hastily returned with his legion in an attempt to protect Londinium and put down the Iceni rebellion. He was able to cobble together his own Legio XIV Gemina (the 14th Legion), parts of Legio XX Valeri Victrix (the 20th Legion), and all available auxiliaries: a total of only 10,000 men. Two other legions were expected to join the fight, but they failed to appear. In the end, Gaius Suetonius had to make do with a mere 10,000 men to face 230,000 Celts.

The Romans were outnumbered twenty-three to one.

C. David Belt

Realizing that he did not have sufficient numbers to defend Londinium, Gaius Suetonius ordered the city to be evacuated. He knew his only chance lay in choosing his battleground carefully, and he could only choose his battleground if he were able to move his army quickly. The Romans, shod with the *caligae*, were able to outdistance and outmaneuver Boudicca's army, which was largely without shoes. Gaius Suetonius marched his legion ahead of the Celts to the West Midlands and positioned his small army inside a natural bowl, shaped like a funnel, near the Roman highway now known as Watling Street. Gaius Suetonius placed his men at the narrow end of the bowl with their backs to a dense forest, leaving them nowhere to retreat. The Romans appeared to be trapped.

And there they waited.

The bait was too great a temptation for Boudicca. She brought her army to the bowl and surrounded it. The Celts were so confident of their impending victory that they brought their women and children in wagons so that the families could watch the slaughter of the hated Romans. Boudicca's forces placed the wagons at the edge of the bowl, hemming in Gaius Suetonius and his vastly outnumbered legion.

When the Celts advanced, the Romans formed up in the nearly impenetrable shield-wall formation known as the *testudo* (tortoise). (See Chapter IV.) Celtic spears and arrows were unable to penetrate the Roman shield-wall. When the Celts advanced to within forty yards of the legion, the Romans threw two volleys of javelins known as *pila*. The *pilum* was designed to bend under its own weight once it struck its target (making it impossible for the enemy to pick up the *pilum* and throw it back). A shield impaled by a *pilum* had to be discarded (because it had a big, heavy, bent iron bar sticking out of it). The first volley of *pila* rendered at most 10,000 Celtic shields useless. The second volley disabled

The Whole Armor of God

more shields. The *pila* attack also destroyed any organized advance by the Celts.

Gaius Suetonius had placed his troops well. Because the Romans were at the narrow end of the bowl, the Celts could not all attack at once. Bracing for the Celtic advance, the Romans at the back of the formation dug in their heels and shoved against the backs of the men in the front ranks. When the Celts collided with shields and swords of the Roman front ranks, the Romans could not be moved. As the battle raged and the ground became soaked with blood (mostly Celtic), the barefoot Celts began to slip and fall in the mud. The Romans, however, shod with hobnailed *caligae*, were able to stand their ground.

With the forces of Boudicca in disarray, the Romans advanced and

attacked in small armored units. As Celtic losses mounted, Boudicca's forces attempted to retreat, but they were trapped inside the bowl: trapped by their own ring of wagons. They had nowhere to go.

C. David Belt

In the end, it was a massacre. One account of the battle tells of 80,000 Celts dead, compared to only 400 Roman casualties. Though outnumbered twenty-three to one, the Romans prevailed.

Had Gaius Suetonius met the Celts on open ground, the Romans would have been surrounded and overwhelmed by the sheer numbers of the enemy. They would have been slaughtered. However, Gaius Suetonius Paulinus was able to move and position his troops in such a way that the superior armor, weapons, and tactics of the Romans won the day.

The battle and the war were won primarily in the *preparation*, because the Romans were able to be *where* they needed to be, *when* they needed to be there. And when the battle was joined, the Romans, unlike the Celts, were able to *stand their ground*. They could not be moved from their chosen place.

Similarly, if we are *prepared*, we will be able to go where the Lord calls us to go, when He calls us to go. It does not matter how great the number of the enemy or how few our numbers. When the foe presses against us, as long as we are on the Lord's errand, having our feet shod with the preparation of the gospel of peace, with our brothers and sisters bracing and pushing behind, we shall be able to stand our ground.

Chapter IV: Scutum

"Above all, taking the shield of faith, wherewith ye shall be able to quench all the fiery darts of the wicked." (*King James Bible*, Ephesians 6:16)

The *scutum* was the shield of the legionnaire. In Paul's time, it was a large, deeply curved, oval shield, made of thick, stout wood, with a metal boss (*umbo*) in the center. The shield was covered with leather or linen. The rim of the *scutum* was protected with leather or metal (steel or bronze). The best surviving example of a *scutum* from this period is 42 inches tall, 26 inches wide, with a distance around the curve of 34 inches. The *scutum* was constructed of three planks of wood glued together to a thickness of about a quarter of an inch. It was light enough to be wielded in one hand and large enough to protect the whole body of the Roman soldier if he crouched behind it. The metal boss protected the hand which held the shield. The boss also protruded from the front of the *scutum* so that the wielder could use the shield to punch his opponent.

As the Romans advanced on the enemy, they would often beat the front of their shields with their swords. Due to the curved shape of the *scutum*, this made a terrible noise. The din of thousands of shields being struck in concert often unnerved the enemy.

The motif painted on the front of the shield identified the military unit (*centuria* or *cohort*). In the confusion of battle, a Roman soldier separated from his unit could quickly recognize members of his own *centuria* or *cohort* and rejoin them.

The Whole Armor of God

On the back of the *scutum*, many legions carried a small quiver of five *plumbatae* (darts). A dart of this era was not a small projectile that could put out an eye; it was a short but lethal javelin with a barbed iron head, weighted with a lump of lead (*plumb*, thus the name *plumbata*), on a short wooden shaft with leather fletchings. *Plumbatae* were thrown in the manner of a German stick grenade *en masse* for a distance of up to seventy-seven yards. The lead weight and the fletching caused the *plumbatae* to rain down with deadly effectiveness, punching through any armor. And unlike arrows shot from a bow, where the bowstrings made a sound, the *plumbata* made no sound at all. In other words, you couldn't hear them coming.

Similar darts were employed by many armies of the ancient world, from the days of the classical Greek civilization through the fall of the Roman Empire. The only defense against such "fiery darts" thrown by the enemy was the shield or *scutum*.

C. David Belt

The Romans employed a shield-wall formation known as the *testudo* (tortoise). Each *centuria* would lock their shields together, with the front rank holding their *scuta* vertically in front while the back ranks held their shields overhead horizontally ("above all"). This created an impenetrable wall that spears, darts, and arrows could not pierce. The *centuria* could move together in the *testudo* formation in what has been described as a "Roman tank." In this manner they could march right over or through the enemy ranks or approach the walls of hostile fortifications with near impunity.

However, once in position inside the *testudo*, the legionnaire was blind. He could not see the enemy or the incoming missiles. And he could not hear them coming. He had to place his trust in the commands of his *centurion* (commander of a *centuria*) or *optio* (chosen officer, the second-in-command). The commander stood with his head exposed above the shield-wall (in many ways making him the bravest man in the unit). The commander became the eyes and ears of the *centuria*. He would give the order to advance, retreat, move left, or move right. He would say when it was safe to lower the shields and throw a volley of *plumbatae* or *pila*.

The Whole Armor of God

Imagine for a moment the terror of huddling under the shield-wall, waiting for the darts to rain death down upon you. You cannot see. You cannot hear. Only the commander can see and hear. And you must trust in him. You must not part the shields and peek. For if you do, the darts will get through and you or someone close to you will die.

Alma said, "And now as I said concerning faith—faith is not to have a perfect knowledge of things; therefore if ye have faith ye hope for things which are not seen, which are true" (Alma 32:21). Paul said, "Now faith is the substance of things hoped for, the evidence of things not seen" (*King James Bible*, Hebrews 11:1). If we, like Roman soldiers, place our shields of faith "above all," we are placing our absolute trust in the Savior, our Commander. We cannot see the incoming darts of the wicked; only He can. The Lord Jesus Christ placed Himself in danger, like a *Centurion* raising His head above the safety of the shields, so that He can guide us, keep us safe, and ultimately, lead us to victory.

However, in order to remain safe behind our shield of faith, we must follow His commands explicitly. As James said, "Even so faith, if it hath not works, is dead, being alone" (James 2:17). If faith is to protect us, we must obey the commandments that will lead us over and through the enemy.

As a member of the Tabernacle Choir at Temple Square, I am blessed to sing with some very talented musicians. Some of them are professional musicians. Some of them are composers and arrangers and choral conductors. Some of them have solo recording careers. But when we enter the choir loft, we set all egos aside. We surrender all control to the conductor. We do not offer suggestions. We do not see what he sees and hear what he hears. We simply follow his directions and his baton. And when we do, when we surrender our will to his, miracles happen.

As modern Christians, we don't like the phrase "blind faith." We shy away from it. We become defensive when it is suggested that we may be following blindly. We say such things as, "No, it's not blind faith. It's *informed* faith." But blind faith is exactly what Paul is suggesting. He is suggesting that we need to surrender our will to the Commander who can see the battlefield as we, ourselves, cannot. We must surrender our will to the One who is our spiritual eyes and ears. And we must do so without peeking, without parting the shields and demanding to see as he sees. Because, if you part the shields when the darts are coming, someone dies. We must trust in His voice, and then and only then will we be safe.

Chapter V: Galea

"And take the helmet of salvation." (*King James Bible*, Ephesians 6:17)

Galea is Latin for helmet. In the first century, Roman helmets appear to have varied widely in style, although the "Imperial Gallic" style of *galea* was the most common type used in the latter half of the first century A.D. These helmets were constructed of iron or mild steel (trimmed with brass) or of bronze. In some cases, they were covered with gold. They were often custom-made for the legionnaire, although some were mass-produced. The *galea* pictured

here is a modern replica of the helmet of an *optio* (chosen officer) and is of the Imperial Gallic style designated as "Type G." (The name "Imperial Gallic" and the "Type G" designation are modern archeological terms.) This style was in common use during the period of Paul's first imprisonment in Rome (a likely time for the writing of the Epistle to the Ephesians).

The *galea* was round, with cheek guards on the side and a neck guard on the back. It had a "brow ridge" on the front. This ridge guarded the face against attacks from above, while keeping the face open. This allowed the Roman soldier an unrestricted field of view and plenty of oxygen. The ears were also left open but protected by ear guards. This design allowed the legionnaire to hear the orders of his commander in the chaos of combat. A crest of dyed horsehair on the top of the *galea* indicated military rank. The *optio* wore his crest longitudinally (i.e., running from front to back). A *centurion* wore his crest transversely (i.e., running from side to side). The rank-and-file legionnaire wore no crest, although many *galea* were equipped with crest holders, because at any time, any legionnaire might be chosen as an *optio*. The *galea* was held in place by being tied under the chin. The helmet was padded inside with fur or a simple wad of rags.

In Paul's time, the brain was understood to be the source of reason and understanding (while the heart was the source of wisdom, the bowels were the seat of mercy and compassion, and the loins the source of vigor and strength). The *galea* protected the soldier's ability to think and reason. Since the brow ridge protected his face, he was able to see clearly and breathe freely. The ear guards protected his ears while enabling him to hear and obey his commander. This ability to

The Whole Armor of God

see, listen, understand, and obey was essential to the survival of the soldier.

On April 2nd, 1972, USAF Lt. Colonel Iceal "Gene" Hambleton, call-sign "Bat-Two-One Bravo," was shot down behind enemy lines during the "Easter Offensive" of the Vietnam War. After five aircraft were lost, sixteen aircraft damaged, at least eleven airmen killed, and two more captured in failed attempts to rescue Lt. Colonel Hambleton, it was determined that a rescue by air was impossible. Lt. Colonel Hambleton was trapped behind enemy lines during the largest armed operation of the war. In order to get to safety, "Bat-Two-One Bravo" was going to have to walk out, through territory controlled by the North Vietnamese Army. The NVA knew who Hambleton was and knew that he had detailed knowledge of Strategic Air Command operations. They wanted him very badly and were actively searching for him.

Since the enemy could hear all transmissions, an *ad hoc* (spur-of-the-moment) code was improvised to guide Hambleton to a point where he could be safely extracted. This code consisted of contemporary cultural jargon and golf references. (Hambleton was an avid golfer and knew many golf courses, quite literally, by heart.) The initial transmission was "You're going to play eighteen holes and you're going to get in the Suwanee and make like Esther Williams and Charlie the Tuna. The round starts on No. 1 at Tucson National."

Hambleton initially responded with, "What have you been smoking?" But he quickly broke the code. "It took me a half-hour to figure out they were giving me distance and direction," Hambleton recalled. "No. 1 at Tucson National is 408 yards running southeast. They wanted me to move southeast 400 yards. The 'course' would lead me to water."

Following these instructions and others like it, Hambleton was able to rendezvous with an allied commando team twelve days after being shot down. His journey was fraught with danger, hand-to-hand combat, starvation, and sickness—he lost forty-five lbs. and broke his arm—but he was rescued. Lt. Colonel Hambleton's ability to listen to the coded instructions and to reason and decipher the *ad hoc* code enabled him to reach safety.

In much the same way, we must listen to the orders of our Commander. We must study His word so that we may understand it. Then we must obey it. If we do, He will lead us to salvation.

One more bit of symbolism to consider: the crest on the top of the *galea* indicated that the soldier was an officer—either a centurion or a chosen

The Whole Armor of God

officer (*optio*). The crest also made the wearer a target. It was a mark of courage to wear the crest. As mentioned earlier, any legionnaire could be chosen as an *optio*. Even if he did not wear a crest, his helmet was often equipped with a crest holder. If an *optio* fell in battle (or was removed from office for misconduct), each man in the unit had to be ready and fit to perform as an *optio*, even at a moment's notice. Likewise, we must be ready and worthy to perform in whatever office we are called to. It is not our place to seek after a particular calling. It is up to the Commander to decide where and how each of us will serve, but we should be ever ready, willing, and worthy to serve. And we must have the courage to carry the crest of our office, to be a target for those who question the wisdom of our Commander and those He has chosen to lead us in His name.

Chapter VI: Gladius

"And the sword of the Spirit, which is the word of God." (*King James Bible*, Ephesians 6:17)

After the Christian soldier is armored, last of all, he takes up the sword.

Gladius Hispaniensis means Spanish sword in Latin and refers to the type of sword the Roman army adopted from the Celtiberians (a Celtic-speaking people who lived in what is now Spain) during the Roman conquest of Hispania. (Even the word *gladius* is very likely derived from a Celtic word, *kladimos*.) Today, the term *gladius* (one of the Latin words for sword) is synonymous with the *gladius Hispaniensis*. The *gladius* was the primary weapon of the legionnaire.

The *gladius* was a short, two-edged sword with a rhomboid cross-section and a tapered point. The blade was typically fashioned out of a single piece of high-carbon steel, although some were created by welding together five layers of steel of varying carbon content. The *gladius* had a solid wooden grip with finger ridges (to allow a sure grasp), a brass-covered oval hilt (to protect the hand), and a round pommel (to provide balance). In Paul's time, two basic styles were in use: the Maintz and the Pompeii. The Maintz blade narrowed slightly in the middle and had a longer point. The Pompeii had a straighter and shorter blade with a shorter point. The example pictured here is of the Pompeii

The Whole Armor of God

style. This style could be mass-produced more quickly than the Maintz. It was more common in the provinces and on the frontier and was just as effective in combat. This was the style with which Paul's audience would have been most familiar.

The Roman soldier carried the *gladius* on a baldric (a leather strap or belt that went over the shoulder) with the sheath over the right (or perhaps left) hip. There is some dispute as to which side was used, but it is generally understood that the centurion and the *optio* wore their swords on the opposite side as a mark of distinction.

Although the *gladius* could be used as a slashing or cutting weapon, it was primarily used as a *thrusting* sword. Typically, the Roman soldier would lead or push with the *scutum* (shield) and then stab with the *gladius*. With its sharp point, the sword slid between plates of armor, piercing with lethal efficiency. Sharpened on both edges, the *gladius* not only stabbed the enemy, it sliced as it penetrated.

In the scriptures, the imagery of a two-edged sword is used a number of times as symbolic of the Spirit and the word of God.

"Behold, I am God; give heed to my word, which is quick and powerful, sharper than a two-edged sword, to the dividing asunder of both joints and marrow; therefore, give heed unto my word" (D&C 6:2). (See also 11:2, 12:2, 14:2, and 33:1 for identical or similar wording.)

"For the word of God is quick, and powerful, and sharper than any two-edged sword, piercing even to the dividing asunder of soul and spirit, and of the joints and marrow, and is a discerner of the thoughts and intents of the heart" (*King James Bible*, Hebrews 4:12).

The apostle John goes so far as to symbolically describe the Lord as having a two-edged sword proceeding out His mouth: "And he had in his right hand seven stars: *and out of his mouth went a sharp twoedged sword*: and his countenance was as the sun shineth

The Whole Armor of God

in his strength" (*King James Bible*, Revelation 1:16, *emphasis added*). (See also 2:12, and 19:21.)

In D&C 27:18, where the Lord reiterates the whole armor of God analogy, He says, "And take the helmet of salvation, and *the sword of my Spirit, which I will pour out upon you, and my word which I reveal unto you*, and be agreed as touching all things whatsoever ye ask of me, and be faithful until I come, and ye shall be caught up, that where I am ye shall be also. Amen" (*emphasis added*).

In *The Book of Mormon*, 3 Nephi 11:3, Mormon describes a voice that pierced "to the center": "And it came to pass that while they were thus conversing one with another, they heard a voice as if it came out of heaven; and they cast their eyes round about, for they understood not the voice which they heard; and it was not a harsh voice, neither was it a loud voice; *nevertheless, and notwithstanding it being a small voice it did pierce them that did hear to the center*, insomuch that there was no part of their frame that it did not cause to quake; yea, it did pierce them to the very soul, and did cause their hearts to burn" (*emphasis added*).

In Alma 31:5, Mormon compares the preaching of the word of God to the sword: "And now, as *the preaching of the word* had a great tendency to lead the people to do that which was just—*yea, it had had more powerful effect upon the minds of the people than the sword*, or anything else, which had happened unto them—therefore Alma thought it was expedient that they should try the virtue of the word of God" (*emphasis added*).

In the book of Alma, we read how Ammon taught the gospel to Lamoni, King in the land of Ishmael. Lamoni was so struck by the Spirit that he was physically overcome and fainted to the earth as if he were dead. When he arose days later, he was converted to the Lord. The same happened when Aaron preached to Lamoni's father, the king of the Lamanites. The old king was touched by the Spirit, collapsed, and rose again, as a new man. In both instances, the Spirit pierced them to the heart, slaying the natural man, leaving a spiritual man to arise.

Korean is a very difficult language for an English-speaking missionary to learn. When my fellow young missionaries and I arrived in South Korea, we were barely able to communicate in the language. We all struggled, but none more so than Elder Guy Pacheco. In those days, as part of the application process, all prospective missionaries took a test to determine how adept we were at learning new languages. While I scored fairly high on the test, Elder Pacheco scored extremely low. (He told me that he scored a zero on the test.) He struggled with the language for his entire mission. Teaching was laborious for him, and those he taught struggled to understand what he said. And yet, he was one of the most successful missionaries in the mission. Why? Because he taught with the Spirit. He was so humble and so earnest as he struggled to speak that those who listened to him were pierced to their very souls.

In Paul's analogy of the whole armor of God, the sword is the only **offensive** weapon. All other items (the belt, the breastplate, the shoes, the shield, and the helmet) are used to protect the Christian soldier. However, the *gladius* is used to attack the enemy. The word of God, when carried by the Spirit, divides asunder both joint and marrow, piercing to the very center. In other words, the witness of the Spirit is not hindered by barriers of flesh and bone ("joint and marrow") but goes straight to the heart. The Spirit speaks directly to our spirits. It touches us on a level that surpasses the flesh.

When so pierced and converted, the enemy of God becomes as dead in the flesh, but arises alive in the Spirit. He or she is no longer an enemy, but a brother or sister in the Church of Jesus Christ.

The Whole Armor of God

Conclusion: Stand

"And having done all, to stand." (*King James Bible*, Ephesians 6:13)

So, we gird ourselves with the truth of who we are and who we represent, armor ourselves with righteousness, prepare ourselves to be where we are supposed to be, when we are supposed to be there, make faith our shield, study, observe, listen, and comprehend the doctrines and commandments of salvation, and speak the word of God with the Spirit. But to what end?

If a Roman legionnaire wore all his armor correctly, followed his orders perfectly, and fought valiantly and courageously, was he guaranteed to come through each battle unscathed? Of course not. Valiant and brave soldiers, including righteous members of the Church are wounded and killed in combat. Teancum and Mormon were two such godly warriors who perished in battle.

Did Samuel the Lamanite know, when he got on that wall and prophesied, that the stones and arrows would miss him? The scriptures give no indication that he did. And yet he climbed up on that wall and spoke the word that the Spirit directed. Did Abinadi—already under a death sentence when he

The Whole Armor of God

voluntarily returned to the city of Nephi to call King Noah and his people to repentance for a *second time* — did he believe that he would live to a ripe old age and be able to bounce his grandchildren on his knee? Did Joseph Smith live to guide the saints to the Valley of the Great Salt Lake or help Emma to raise their children? Is every missionary who faithfully serves a mission for the Lord *assured* that he or she will be preserved from danger?

The answer is obviously no. Abinadi was burned at the stake. Joseph Smith rode to Carthage knowing he would die there. Missionaries have been murdered, have been killed in accidents, and have contracted lethal illnesses. Following the commandments of God — even if we could be perfect in our obedience (and none of us are) — does not guarantee physical safety.

After all, the Savior led a sinless life and He was crucified. "The Son of Man hath descended below them all. Art thou greater than he?" (D&C 122:8)

So why do we put on the whole armor of God?

C. David Belt

We put on the whole armor of God to protect ourselves from *spiritual* danger. "Put on the whole armour of God, that ye may be able to stand against the wiles of the devil. For we wrestle not against flesh and blood, but against principalities, against powers, against the rulers of the darkness of this world, against spiritual wickedness in high places" (*King James Bible*, Ephesians 6:11–12). The true danger is not physical, but spiritual in nature. But unlike a Roman soldier who dons his physical armor of iron, steel, wood and leather, if we put on the whole armor of God, we are *guaranteed* spiritual safety. Even if we perish in the flesh, we will have life eternal.

If we place ourselves in the Lord's hands, He *will* protect us. "Fear thou not; for I am with thee: be not dismayed; for I am thy God: I will strengthen thee; yea, I will help thee; yea, I will uphold thee with the right hand of my righteousness" (*King James Bible*, Isaiah 41:10). These words of the Lord as spoken by Isaiah have been inspiringly set to music in the hymn, "How Firm a Foundation." The final verse of that hymn expresses eloquently that the Savior will never abandon us:

> *The soul that on Jesus hath leaned for repose*
> *I will not, I cannot, desert to his foes;*
> *That soul, though all hell should endeavor to shake,*
> *I'll never, no never, I'll never, no never,*
> *I'll never, no never, no never forsake!* [2]

---

[2] "How Firm a Foundation," *Hymns no. 85, v. 7*. Text: attributed to Robert Keen, ca. 1787. Music: Anon., ca. 1889.

The Whole Armor of God

Putting on the *whole* armor of God requires us to do *all* that we can do. Half measures and incomplete commitment cannot protect us. Simply declaring that we come in the name of the Lord God by wearing our spiritual *cingulum militare* will not protect us from the assault of the enemy. Wearing a *lorica segmentata* of righteousness alone will not protect us from all danger, because our own righteousness is never sufficient or perfect. Without a *galea* of salvation, we cannot understand what it is we are required to do. Wearing a *galea* and a *lorica segmentata* will not stop the darts of the wicked; for that, we must also wield the *scutum* of faith and surrender our will to our Commander. If we are not in the right place at the right time by wearing the *caligae* of the preparation of the gospel of peace, we will be overrun and overwhelmed, and we *will* fall. And if we attempt to attack the enemy using any weapon other than the word of God as confirmed by the Spirit, we will not pierce the soul of the enemy.

As Paul said, we must put on the *whole* armor of God so that, "having done all," we will be able "to stand" (*King James Bible*, Ephesians 6:13). In other words, once we have done all that God requires of us, we will be upheld by His righteous hand, and we will be victorious.

Acknowledgments

You can blame this whole project on my mom.

It was her idea. She suggested it as a way to combine five of my passions: history, ancient weaponry, storytelling, scriptural symbolism, and love for my Savior. She also wanted me to have an outlet for my writing that I could pursue on the sabbath day. In addition, she proofread and critiqued every word. So, to my mother, Mable F. Belt, I wish to express my profound gratitude. Cindy L. Belt, my dear, lovely eternal companion has been my muse throughout this entire process. She is and has been my first line of defense and, like my mother, has proofread and critiqued every word I've ever written for publication. Jacob M. Belt, my youngest son, was a great sport as he portrayed my legionnaire, a role he continues to play in my many "Whole Armour of God" firesides. Olya Polazhynets Goodrick, my almost-daughter, traveled all the way from Texas to do the photography. Bryan J. Belt served as Olya's assistant on the photo shoot. Other proofreaders included Bryan J. Belt, Jenny Flake Rabe, Amber Hall, and many others from the LDS Beta Readers group. Eric D. Huntsman, PhD, has been my long-suffering resource on many writing projects, and he was invaluable on this one. We sometimes sit together in the Tabernacle Choir at Temple Square, and I am always peppering him with questions about Latin, Roman history, and ancient scripture. His foreword added a wonderful new dimension to this work, and I am deeply indebted to him. David Belt (my dad, not me) provided encouragement. He has always encouraged me. Whenever I go off to do a fireside on the Whole Armour of God or teach a class on ancient weaponry, he helps pack and load up my arsenal of eighty-plus pieces, both weaponry and armor. Many times, he has accompanied me on these jaunts, helping with the weapons. And when I return home, he is always there to help unload and carry the entire arsenal back up the stairs to my office. He is a treasure. To him and to all the rest of you, I thank you from the bottoms of my *caligae*.

I also wish to express gratitude to my Heavenly Father and my Lord and Savior, Jesus Christ. I have prayed for guidance on this project. My Father in Heaven has answered my prayers and guided me through His Holy Spirit. None of this would have any meaning, however, without the

The Whole Armor of God

supreme love of Jesus, who suffered and died and rose again that you and I might live again and grow to be perfected in Him.

I know He lives.

C. David Belt

About the Author

C. David Belt was born in the wilds of Evanston, Wyoming. As a child, he lived and traveled extensively around the Far East. In Thailand, he once fed so many bananas to a monkey, the poor creature swore off bananas for life. He served as a missionary in South Korea and southern California (Korean-speaking), and yes, he loves kimchi. He graduated from Brigham Young University with a BS in Computer Science and a minor in Aerospace Studies, but he managed to bypass all English and writing classes. He served as a B-52 pilot in the US Air Force and as an Air Weapons Controller in the Washington Air National Guard and was deployed to locations so secret, his family still does not know where he risked life and limb (other than in an 192' wingspan aircraft flying 200' off the ground in mountainous terrain). When he is not writing, he sings in the Tabernacle Choir at Temple Square and works as a software engineer. He collects swords, spears, and axes (oh, my!), and other medieval weapons and armor. He and his wife have six children (and a growing number of grandchildren) and live in Utah with an eclectus parrot named Mork (who likes to jump on the keyboard when David is writing). There is also a cat, but she can't be bothered to take notice of the parrot, and so that is all the mention we shall make of her.

C. David Belt is the author of *The Children of Lilith* trilogy, *The Sweet Sister*, *Time's Plague*, and *The Arawn Prophecy*. For more information, please visit www.unwillingchild.com.

About the Photographer

Olya Polazhynets Goodrick was born and raised in the Transcarpathian region of Ukraine where she attended art school. She was an exchange student in the US during her senior year in high school and then moved across the Atlantic to pursue an education at Brigham Young University in Provo, UT. Since then she's gotten married, moved around a bit, and is (for now) settled in the Panhandle of Texas. Even though Olya graduated with a major in Russian Language and Literature and a minor in Physics, she's always had a love for art in general and photography in particular. Recently, she's been working as a visual media designer for Core Focus, Inc. and in various other creative projects.

About the Legionnaire

Jacob M. Belt enjoys extreme sports workouts and someday hopes to compete on American Ninja Warrior. He enjoys watching and collecting movies, and his collection exceeds eight hundred titles (as of last count). He currently resides in the Salt Lake Valley with his lovely wife and goofy Labrador. He loves video games, playing frisbee golf, and watching the Seahawks. He also has a small collection of medieval weaponry, with a focus on the Viking era.

About Dr. Huntsman

Eric Huntsman, with a PhD in Ancient History from the University of Pennsylvania, is a Professor of Ancient Scripture at Brigham Young University, where he directs the program in Ancient Near Eastern Studies. His research and writing focus on the New Testament and Judaism and Christianity in the Roman World.

www.ingramcontent.com/pod-product-compliance
Lightning Source LLC
Chambersburg PA
CBHW061252040426
42444CB00010B/2361